Taylor Swift
Country Music Star

Maggie Murphy

PowerKiDS press.

New York

To Maud, who loves Taylor Swift as much as I do

Published in 2011 by The Rosen Publishing Group, Inc.
29 East 21st Street, New York, NY 10010

First Edition

Book Design: Greg Tucker
Photo Researcher: Jessica Gerweck

Library of Congress Cataloging-in-Publication Data

Murphy, Maggie.
    Taylor Swift : country music star / Maggie Murphy. — 1st ed.
        p. cm. — (Young and famous)
    Includes index.
    ISBN 978-1-4488-0645-4 (library binding) —
    ISBN 978-1-4488-1803-7 (pbk.) — ISBN 978-1-4488-1804-4 (6-pack)
    1. Swift, Taylor, 1989—Juvenile literature. 2. Women country musicians—United States—Biography—Juvenile literature. I. Title.
    ML3930.S989M87 2011
    782.421642092—dc22
    [B]
                        2009047937

Manufactured in the United States of America

CPSIA Compliance Information: Batch #WS10PK: For Further Information contact Rosen Publishing, New York, New York at 1-800-237-9932

Contents

Taylor Swift is a country music star.

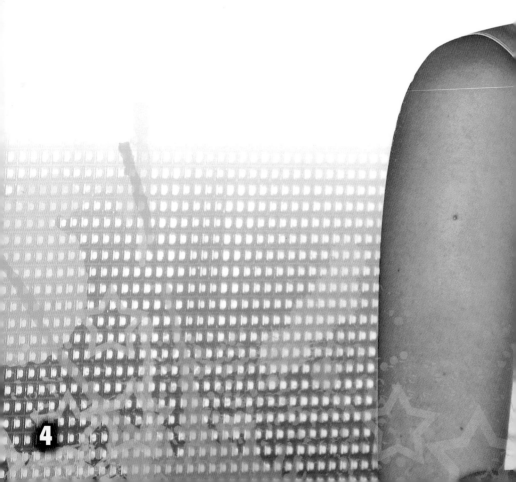

Taylor lives near Nashville, Tennessee. Many country stars live near Nashville.

Taylor sings and writes songs. She also plays guitar and piano.

The albums *Taylor Swift* and *Fearless* were Taylor's big hits. They made her **famous**.

Some of Taylor's songs are about love. Others are about boys and high school.

Taylor plays a lot of **concerts**. Many of her fans come to see her **perform**.

Taylor's fans
love her music.

Taylor has won many **awards**. She won an MTV Video Music Award in 2009.

Taylor has acted in movies. She was in *Valentine's Day*.

Taylor loves to make music. She will be famous for a long time.

Books

Here are more books to read about Taylor Swift:

Rawson, Katherine. *Taylor Swift*. Kid Stars! New York: Power Kids Press, 2010.

Reusser, Kayleen. *Taylor Swift*. Hockessin, DE: Mitchell Lane Publishers, 2008.

Web Sites

Due to the changing nature of Internet links, PowerKids Press has developed an online list of Web sites related to the subject of this book. This site is updated regularly. Please use this link to access the list:
www.powerkidslinks.com/young/ts/

Glossary

awards (uh-WORDZ) Honors given to people.

concerts (KONT-serts) Public musical performances.

famous (FAY-mus) Very well known.

perform (per-FORM) To sing, dance, act, or play music in front of other people.

Index